The Power of Agreement
GLOBAL PRAYER NETWORK
Prayer Guide

Mother Artherrine Grimes Hoskins

Copyright © 2019 by Evangelist Artherrine Grimes-Hoskins

All Rights reserved. No part of this book may be reproduced or transmitted in any form or by any means, electronic or mechanical, including photocopying, recording, or by any information storage and retrieval system, without permission in writing from the copyright owner.

This book was printed in the United States of America.

"If My people who are called by My name will humble themselves, and pray and seek My face, and turn from their wicked ways, then I will hear from heaven, and will forgive their sin and heal their land."
2 Chronicles 7:14, NKJV

DEDICATION

This book is dedicated to My Heavenly Father, Jehovah God who gave me the vision for my first published work. Thank You for stirring me and making it obvious to me that I should do this project, *NOW!* To my Savior and Lord Jesus Christ of Nazareth, who is my chief intercessor and High Priest (Hebrew 10:10). Thank You, Lord Jesus Christ! To God Be the Glory!

To the memory of beloved my parents, Arthur Lee and Francis Lowe Aiden Grimes. I knowledge my love and gratitude for always being there for me. Thanks for teaching me God's wisdom, godly fear and how to pray. So grateful.

To my husband, Harvey Eugene Hoskins of over 42 years, you have truly been my friend, encourager, supporter, and a stabilizing force in my life. Thank you for being with me and for me. Thank you for being so patient with me. You have always inspired me beyond what I thought I could do. Only Our Heavenly Father, Jehovah knows how I love and appreciate you. So grateful.

To my precious children, Kimberly, Damon, Harlan, Kendall, and Anna Hoskins, thanks for your encouragement and inspiration. To my motivators, my six grandchildren, Nia, Jayla, Nazyr, Keanna, Kamora and Kendall Jr., thanks for your love and hugs. My siblings, Theresa, Alton, Nina B, Travis, and Terry, thanks for always supporting and believing in me. Thanks to Mother Mary Mimms, who taught me to pray the WORD of God and to remain faithful to God. Thank you to all my extended family for your love. So grateful.

ACKNOWLEDGEMENTS

This is my first publication. I am deeply grateful for everyone who has assisted me in the completion of this book. I am pleased to acknowledge them and their invaluable contributions. I would like to thank each Warrior who contributed prayers for this project; Warrior Minister Crystal Bouldin, Warrior Catherine Floyd, Warrior Minister Desmarie Guyton, Warrior Pastor Deborah Holt-Foster, Warrior Joan Vanleer Moore, Warrior Husband Harvey E. Hoskins, CPA, Warrior Gwelthalyn Huff, Warrior Pastor Terrell Hunt, Warrior Pastors Chris and Gina Inkum, Warrior Pastor Pamela G. Kellar, Warrior Prophet Mark Korley, Warrior Apostle Eugenie Angela Mayers, Warrior Antonia McLaurin, Warrior Sharon Mitchell, Warrior Mother Kathleen Talley, Warrior Gloria Towner, Warrior Mother Gloria Wigfall, Warrior Dr. Diana R. Williams, and Warrior Gloria Wise, Dr Peggy Enoch, and Thanks to Warrior Jacqui Rogers, and Minister/Coach Yolanda E. Shields for guiding me through the ups and downs of book updates for publishing

In the preparation of the manuscript, I am indebted to Reverend Dr. Diana R. Williams for her proofreading and sharing her knowledge and talents of publishing, and Pastor Pamela G. Kellar for contributing your design and layout skills and sharing your knowledge in printing/publishing.

To all of the Prayer Warriors for the Power of Agreement Global Prayer Network Ministry all over the United States, Africa (Ghana), Jamaica, Israel, Mexico, Switzerland, Bahamas and Barbados, that pray as a community of love and unity on the Power of Agreement prayer lines. Thanks for your prayers and participation.

Finally, a special thanks to Reverend Willie McLaurin and the Tennessee Baptist Mission Board for your fervent prayers and generous support.

All scriptures are reference in the King James Version except when noted. A variety of Bible versions were chosen for clarification purposes. Although the Bible must never be mishandled by private interpretations, the author's insights can be obscured by failing to select the words that explain the points emphasized. We pray that each version examined add an element of personal revelation to the reader. Each version used and its abbreviations are listed below in alphabetical order.

AMP—Scripture is taken from the Amplified Bible, Old Testament © 1965, 1987 by the Zondervan Corporation the Amplified New Testament © 1958, 1987 by the Lockman Foundation. Used by permission.

AMPC—Amplified Bible, Classic Edition Copyright © 1954, 1958, 1962, 1964, 1965, 1987 by The Lockman Foundation

CEV—Contemporary English Version © 1995 by American Bible Society

CJB—Complete Jewish Bible Copyright © 1998 by David H. Stern. All rights reserved.

KJV—King James Version © 1989 by World Publishing

NIV—New International Version © 1973, 1978, 1984 by International Bible Society

NKJV—New King James Version © 1974, 1978, 1982 by Thomas Nelson, Inc. Publishers

GREETINGS

The Power of Agreement Global Prayer Network (GPN) is over 29 years old. It started out as Greater Nashville Prayer Network. As the Founder/Leader of this organization, I called for the mourning/cunning women to come forth and pray for families/churches and the community in 1987. In 1990 at Rev. Bob Stout's Business Office, we became the Greater Nashville Prayer Network. We were greatly blessed by the teachings on prayer of late Pastor Charles Blackmon and his wife Pastor Linda Blackmon and we continue to hear from her prophetic voice. About nine years ago, the organization became nationally known as Warriors across the United States and began to pray for the first African American President, President Barack H. Obama. About two years ago, it became global under the direction of Pastors Chris and Gina Inkum and Prophet Mark Korley from Ghana.

What Prayer Means to Me & those who have impacted my prayer journey and ministry…

Prayer to me is communicating with our Heavenly Father by speaking and listening, and also getting the earthly permission for heavenly intervention. The Power of Agreement Global Prayer Network (GPN) Ministry is raising up intercessors. Intercessory prayer is the act of praying to God on the behalf of others. Prayer involves repentance, confession, praise, worship, adoration, spiritual warfare and thanksgiving. Spiritual warfare is the concept of fighting against the evil forces; spirits that intervene in human affairs in various ways.

The goal of prayer for GPN is to allow the Holy Spirit to move us beyond "low end" (for example, now I lay me down to sleep…) prayers; up and into high level intercession.

Jesus was empowered for rich kingdom ministry by resting in God's glory and grace while being positioned in love according to Luke 5:15-16 NASB. "But the news about Him was spreading even farther, and large crowds were gathering to hear Him and to be healed of their sicknesses. But Jesus Himself would often slip away to the wilderness and pray." Intercessors, it is time to slip away and pray.

It is my prayer that intercessory prayer will become a reality in your life and in the lives of all those who partake thereof. The best intercession is informed, and spirit led prayers. Therefore, allow the prayer guide to empower your intercession and aid you in assisting in the kingdom work by ushering in the Kingdom of our God and His Son, Our Savior and Lord, Jesus Christ.

Giving praise to the Heavenly Father for the following people that have impacted my prayer journey and ministry: My Great High Priest and perfect example of an intercessor, The Lord Jesus Christ, Charles Spurgeon, John and Charles Wesley, my parents, Arthur Lee & Frances Lowe Grimes, Dr. Myles Munroe, Prayer Warrior Eleanor Graves, Pastor Linda Blackman, Pastor/Dr. Arthur Alexander, Pastor Renee Franklin, Apostle Kimberly Daniels, Mother Mary Mimms, Dr. Cindy Trimm, Prayer Warrior Germaine Copeland, Pastor Glen Clay, Apostle John Eckhardt, Pastor Chris Inkum, Prayer Warrior Stormie Omartian, Pastor/Dr. Diana Williams, Prayer Warrior Sandy Vincent, Bishop Rice Brooks and Pastor James Lowe.

All of the above have mentored me through teachings, intercession, time, prophetic insight or books/CDs. They have had a positive effect on my life and calling as an intercessor.

In His Service
Artherrine Grimes-Hoskins
Founder & Overseer of Power of Agreement (GPN Inc.). Evangelist, Intercessor, Prayer Warrior

Currently, we have about 15 consistent phone lines. For 10 years, we met monthly at Historic First Community Church under the direction of Pastors Glen and Ella Clay. In accordance with the prophecy given by Dr. Sandy Powell of Power House Ministries in 2007, the ministry began to multiply rapidly with women joining the Mother's Line to command and commit their day to the Most High God Jehovah in Jesus name. They prayed for their children and other children in their sphere of influence. Father God Jehovah is continuously opening doors and closing doors for His Glory!

The purpose of this ministry is to teach and impart effective praying. We have two groups of individuals involved; those in training and those of mature levels. We are seeing signs, miracles, and wonders! Since Pastor Yvonne Johnson taught on the subject of angels during a Monday night,

(States/Nation/Nations and President Prayer Line), testimonies have tripled regarding our angels from Jehovah God. *"But the meek (in the end) shall inherit the earth and shall delight themselves in the abundance of peace"*, Psalm 37:11, AMPC. I have written and also compiled prayers written by various prayer leaders within the GPN to bless your prayer life!

So Grateful,
Mother Artherrine Grimes Hoskins
Nashville, TN July 2019

THE PRAYER LINES
615 307-6988
Monday
Mother's Prayer Line– 6:15am-7am CT, 7:15am 8am ET, 4:15am-5am PT
Israel Prayer Line-7:30am-8:30am CT, 8:30am, 9:30 am ET, and 5:30am-6:30am PT
State, President, Nation(s) Prayer Line 7:30pm-8:30pm CT, 8:30 pm-9:30pm ET, 5:30pm-6:30pm PT

Tuesday
Men's Watchmen Prayer Line-7am-7:30am CT, 8 am-8:30am ET, 5am-5:30am PT

Wednesday
Mother's Prayer Line– 6:15am-7am CT 7:15am-8am ET, 4:15am-5am PT
Prayer & Fasting Line-12:15pm-1:15pm CT, 1:15 pm-2:15pm ET, 10:15am-11:15am PT

Thursday
Unmarried Prayer Line-(1st, 3rd, 5th)-7pm-8pm CT, 8pm-9pm ET, 5pm-6pm PT
Children/Youth Lift Me Up (319-527-4787) 6:30pm-7pm CT, 7:30 pm-8pm ET, 4:30pm-5pm PT

Friday
Mother's Prayer Line– 6:15am-7am CT, 7:15am-8am ET, 4:15am-5am PT

Hope & Healing Prayer Line (1st, 3rd, 5th)-7:30-8:30am CT, 8:30-9:30am ET, 5:30-6:30am PT
Widows Prayer Line- (4th) 7:30am-8:30am CT, 8:30 pm-9:30pm ET, 5:30am-6:30am PT

Saturday
Marriage Prayer Line (2nd, 4th) 8:15am-9:15am CT, 9:15am-10:15am ET, 6:15am-7:15am PT

Sunday
Family Prayer Line (2nd) 7:30pm CT, 8:30 pm ET, 5:30pm PT

Push Prayer Line
Monday-Saturday (781-448-0427)
5am-6am CT, 6am-7am PT, 3am-4am PT

"Now this is the confidence that we have in Him, that if we ask anything according to His will, He hears us. And if we know that He hears us, whatever we ask, we know that we have the petitions that we have asked of Him."

1 John 5:14 -15, NKJV

Marching Orders

Call for the Praying/Mourning/Cunning Women of God

By Warrior/Minister Joan Vanleer Moore for the Prayer Network in 1990

Jeremiah 9:17-21
V.17-Thus saith the Lord of Hosts, consider ye, and call for the mourning women, that they may come; and send for cunning women, that they may come:

Original Hebrew
Mourning=quwn (koon)=to strike a musical note, i.e. chant or wail (at a funeral) lament, mourning women.
Cunning +Chokmah (khaw-Kawn)=wise, i.e., intelligent, skillful or artful.
These seem to be two different groups: mourning and cunning women, or either both attributes are to be present within the women that are called to assemble.

V.18 - And let them make haste, and take up a wailing for us, that our eyes may run down with tears, and our eyelids gush out with water.

Wailing nahah (naw haw)=to groan (through the idea of crying aloud), to assemble (as if on proclamation).

V. 19 For a voice of wailing is heard out of Zion: How are we spoiled! We are greatly confounded, because we have forsaken the land, because our dwellings have cast us out.

V.20 Yet hear the word of the Lord, O ye women, and let your ear receive the word of His mouth, and teach your daughters wailing, and every one of her neighbor lamentation.

V.21 For death is come up into our windows, and is entered into our palaces, to cut off the children from without, and the young men from the streets.

A PRAYER OF WORSHIP &

PRAISE UNTO THE LORD OUR GOD

By Prayer Warrior Jacqui Rogers

Heavenly Father, Adonai, El Elyon, Elohim, El Olam, El Roi, El Shaddai, Immanuel, Almighty God, how majestic is your name in all the earth. To the King of Kings, and the Lord of Lords; You are the Alpha and the Omega; the beginning and the end; the first and the last; the one and only true and living God! Full of all power. The Sovereign God of Abraham, Isaac and Jacob, the LORD God of Israel. We magnify your holy name; we pray your will to be done on earth as it is commanded in the heavens, and we thank you for your many, countless blessings that you've bestowed upon those that love, hope and believe in your son, Jesus the Christ! Emmanuel! God with us! Author and Finisher, Bread of Life, Bridegroom, Bright and Morning Star, the Chosen One, the Day Spring, the Deliverer, the Door, the Chief Cornerstone, the Kinsmen Redeemer, the Precious Lamb of God, Lion of the Tribe of Judah, Master, Messiah, Rabboni, The Truth & the Resurrection, Wonderful

Counsellor, Mighty God, Prince of Peace, Everlasting Father; for You and He are as One! And we're grateful for your Holy Spirit that servers as Comforter and Teacher: We bow down and we bless you Abba Father for You are great and greatly to be praised! All the honour, all the praise and all the glory belong to you and we will not give it another!

        HALLELUJAH & AMEN!

PRAYER FOR CLEANSING OF THE HEART
ANONYMOUS

Father God, I stand in Your presence with praise and thanksgiving in my heart in the name of Jesus. I thank You, Father, that I have been washed in the blood of the Lamb and redeemed from the curse of the law. And Father God, this day I choose to behave myself wisely and to give heed to the blameless way. I will walk within my house in integrity and with a blameless heart, I set no base or wicked thing before my eyes. I hate the work of them who turn aside from the right path. It will not, Father, grasp hold. A perverse heart shall depart from me. I will know no evil person or thing.

I take no part in or have fellowship with the fruitless deeds and enterprises of darkness but instead, my life is so in contrast as to expose and reprove and convict them. So, Father this day I choose to be useful, helpful and kind, tenderhearted and compassionate, understanding, loving hearted, forgiving, readily and freely as God and Christ has forgiven me. And Father God, I pray this day that the words of my mouth and the meditation of my heart is acceptable in Your sight, Father. In Jesus name, I pray.

FORGIVENESS PRAYER
By Warrior Dr. Diana R. Williams

"For if you forgive other people when they sin against you, your heavenly Father will also forgive you." Matthew 6:14, NIV

Dear Jehovah – Shalom,

You, Lord are Peace and the Lover of my Soul! I praise Your Holy Name! You know everything about me and when I am hurt. I run to You now for comfort and forgive everyone who has trespassed against me so that YOU can forgive me my trespasses. I pray for all who have wounded and offended me and place their names on the altar (***NAME/S*****).

Please help me to let go of all anger, bitterness, resentment, and unkindness in any form. It was not fair, it was not deserved, it was unexpected, and it did take a toll on me. But, I make the choice today to absolve, let off the hook, pardon, release, and set (initials) free. Instead of continuing to be sad, disappointed, or angry about it, I thank You that I have great peace in this situation. With Your help, I refuse to be hurt, vengeful, enraged, or made to stumble about (initials)'s conduct any longer.

Help me to be compassionate, loving, and merciful toward those who have offended me. From this moment on, I will walk in love with kind and patient behavior. I will not be rude, selfish, or quick-tempered. I am no longer stuck in rumination over wrongs that others do. Instead, I move forward in hope and conduct myself toward (initials) in a manner that is pleasing to You. If at any time bad memories resurface to inflict pain or torment, I will cast my care upon You and pray this forgiveness prayer again. I can do all things – including forgiving others - through Christ. From this day forward, your divine favor surrounds me as a protective shield and I abide safely in Your arms where according to Isaiah 54:17, no weapon formed against me can prosper! In the powerful name of Jesus, I pray. Amen.

PROMISE PRAYER OF PSALM 23
By Apostle Mother Eugenie Angela Mayers

The Lord Jesus Christ is my Shephard.
 I shall not want.
The Lord Jesus Christ makes me to lie down in green pastures.
The Lord Jesus Christ leads me beside the still waters.
The Lord Jesus Christ restores my soul:
The Lord Jesus Christ leads me through the paths of righteousness for the Lord Jesus Christ namesake,
Yea though I walk through the valley of the shadow of death, I will fear no evil: For the Lord Jesus Christ is with me;
The Lord Jesus Christ rod and the Lord Jesus Christ staff they comfort me.
The Lord Jesus Christ prepares a table before me in the presence of my enemies;
The Lord Jesus Christ anoints my head with oil. My cup runs over.
Surely goodness and mercy shall follow me all the days of my life;
and I will dwell in the house of the Lord Jesus Christ forever.

PUT ON THE WHOLE ARMOR OF GOD
By Mother Artherrine Grimes Hoskins

Good Morning Our Heavenly Father! Good Morning Our Lord/Savior Jesus! Good Morning Our Companion Holy Spirit!

We thank You for the Victory for this day! We thank You for allowing us to arise to see another day of new mercies. We cover ourselves with the blood of Jesus and claim the protection of the blood for family, finances, home, business, ministry, spirit, soul and body. We surrender ourselves completely in every area of our lives to You. We will not hate, envy, or show any type of bitterness toward our brothers, sisters, or our enemies, but we will love them with the love of God shed aboard in our hearts by the Holy Ghost. Pour Holy Spirit. Pour Holy Spirit. Pour Holy Spirit. By faith, I/we put on Your full armor right now: By faith, I/we put on your belt of truth to cover our loins according to Psalm 51:6, *"Behold thou desireth truth at the inward parts; and in the hidden part thou shalt make us to know wisdom."*
 May our lives be motivated by truth so that we can maintain integrity. By faith, we put on the breastplate of righteousness to cover our hearts and chest cavities according to 2nd Corinthians 6:7, *"By the word of truth, by the power of God, by the armor of righteousness on the right hand and on the left."*
Thank you for the imputed righteousness of Jesus

Christ. Help us understand that we are righteous to You as Jesus Himself.

By faith, we put on the shoes of the gospel of peace to cover our feet according to Isaiah 52:7, *"How beautiful upon the mountains are the feet of them that bringeth gospel tidings; that publishes peace; that bringeth good tidings; that publishes salvation."* Holy Spirit, help us to stand in Christ Victory this day. Help us be peacemakers and not trouble makers. Help us to bring Your peace to all we encounter today.

By faith, we take the shield of faith to defensively and offensively cover our bodies according to Hebrews 10:38, *"Now the just shall live by faith but if any man/woman draw back, My soul shall have no pleasure in him/her."* Remind us that your protection completely surrounds us even during satan's most vicious attacks. May we trust You and Your WORD today and not add fuel to any satan's darts. Thank You, Father that we can go into this day without fear. By faith, we put on the helmet of Salvation so that we can stay sane and saved according to 1 Thessalonians 5:8, *"But we belong to the day. So we must stay sober and let our faith and love the day/the light, be sober, put on the breastplate of faith and love be like a suit of armor"* (CEV). Our firm hope that we will be saved is our helmet. Help us to live in the future tense. Make us clearly see that we belong to You through Christ's death and that satan can never own us again.

By faith, we take the Sword of the Spirit which is Your WORD according to Ephesians 6:17, "Let God's saving power be like a helmet, and for a sword use God's message that comes from the Spirit" (CEV). Thank You for the precious gift of Your WORD, it is strong and powerful, the defensive weapon to defeat all evil. Help us to remember Your WORD and use it today. Holy Spirit help us never to forget that there is truth in the WORD to defeat every lie satan may ever tell us.

By faith, we add the last piece of armor, praying always with all prayer and supplication for all the saints according to Ephesians 6:18, *"Pray always with all prayer and supplication in the Spirit and to be watchful with all perseverance and supplication for all the saints."* Father, we ask you this day for a new and fresh anointing and to be covered in the blood of Jesus. Yesterday's anointing can't work for the task(s) for this new day. Anointing fall on us!

Now Heavenly Father, we praise You and we thank You for the armor You have provided for us to dress in this day. Thank You Father, we are completely covered now, in the name of Jesus, in the blood of Jesus, and according to Your WORD.

Father, we are Yours. Father rise up big today within us. In the matchless, mighty name of the Lord Jesus Christ of Nazareth, Amen

COMMANDING THE MORNING

One can discover the secrets of doing exploits for God by specifically decreeing and declaring a thing and commanding our day. There will be an improvement in the way you think, talk, live, pray and believe. Commanding your morning can release overcoming power in your heart. You can take charge of your day by commanding your morning. We can take control of our destinies by learning to command our mornings. Command means to order with authority, to take charge of, and to guard.

> …set your words in order before me; take your stand – Job 33:5.
>
> Ephesians 6:14, 18 (NLT) Stand your ground… Stay alert and be persistent in your prayers…

As a born-again believer of the Lord Jesus Christ, you have been commanded by God to have authority and power. We have been empowered by the Lord Jesus Christ to exercise authority over the sun, moon, the stars and all of the elements of heaven. God has put all things under your control (Ps. 8:6)

Our survival in the last days depends on deep warfare prayers. Jesus would spend time in prayer to establish God's divine agenda in the earth realm. Jesus dislodged evil and downloaded victory, success and prosperity in His day. He was exposing His disciples to the discipline of Kingdom living.

To command means to keep watch, regulate, give orders to; Instruct, dictate, exercise authority, decree, control, supervise.

Let us ask Jesus like the disciples did in Luke 11:1; Lord Jesus teach us how to pray your type of prayers; teach us how to obtain results in prayer. Teach us how to command the morning and the day. Teach us how to speak so that the whole creation will listen and obey. The daily affirmations of Jesus in Luke 11 cannot work until we command them into action.

Many have died before their destinies are met; many have died before their time (premature deaths). The majority of the problems encountered during our day could be averted if we would take the time to command our morning.

The enemy knows how important the morning is. The reason the enemy introduces distractions into our lives is because he knows the importance of commanding our mornings.

Be mindful that the morning is the beginning of the day and of life. Therefore, learn to command your morning and you will get what you speak.

Artherrine Grimes-Hoskins
Founder & Overseer of Power of Agreement (GPN, Inc)
Evangelist, Intercessor and Prayer Warrior

PRAYER POINTS TO COMMAND YOUR MORNING

By praying these Prayer Points, you can deprogram any evil programmed against you. Start by singing songs of Praises and Thanksgiving to God for giving you another new day! I encourage you to form the habit of prevailing in prayer over the enemies on a daily basis.

- I TAKE AUTHORITY OVER THIS DAY IN THE NAME OF JESUS!
- I CONFESS THAT THIS IS THE DAY THAT THE LORD HAS MADE, I WILL REJOICE AND BE GLAD IN IT, IN THE NAME OF JESUS!
- I DRAW UPON HEAVENLY FORCES TODAY, IN THE NAME OF JESUS! O DAY, ARISE AND GIVE ME MY PORTION IN JESUS NAME!
- I DECREE AND DECLARE THAT ALL THE ELEMENTS OF THIS DAY WILL COOPERATE WITH ME, IN JESUS NAME!
- I DECREE AND DECLARE THAT THESE ELEMENTAL FORCES WILL REFUSE TO COOPERATE WITH MY ENEMIES THIS DAY, IN JESUS NAME!

- I SPEAK UNTO YOU THE SUN, MOON AND THE STARS, YOU WILL NOT SMITE ME AND MY FAMILY THIS DAY, IN JESUS NAME!
- I PULL DOWN EVERY NEGATIVE ENERGY PLANNING TO OPERATE AGAINST MY LIFE THIS DAY, IN JESUS NAME!
- I RENDER NULL AND VOID INCANTATIONS AND SANTANIC PRAYER OVER ME AND MY FAMILY, IN JESUS NAMES!
- LET EVERY BATTLE IN THE HEAVENLIES BE WON IN FAVOR OF THE ANGELS CONVEYING MY BLESSINGS TODAY, IN THE NAME OF JESUS!
- O SUN, MOON AND STARS, CARRY YOUR AFFLICTIONS BACK TO THE SENDER, AND RELEASE THEM AGAINST HIM/HER, IN THE NAME OF JESUS!
- O GOD, ARISE AND UPROOT EVERTHING YOU HAVE NOT PLANTED IN THE HEAVENLIES THAT IS WORKING AGAINST ME, IN JESUS NAME!
- LET THE WICKED BE SHAKEN OUT FROM THE END OF THE EATH, IN THE NAME OF JESUS!

- O SUN, AS YOU COME FORTH, UPROOT ALL THE WICKEDNESS THAT HAS COME AGAINST MY LIFE IN JESUS NAME!
- I PROGRAM BLESSINGS UNTO THE SUN, MOON AND THE STARS FOR MY LIFE TODAY, IN THE NAME OF JESUS!
- O SUN, MOON AND STARS FIGHT AGAINST THE STRONGHOLD OF WITCHCRAFT TARGETED AGAINST ME TODAY IN THE NAME OF JESUS!
- O HEAVENS, FIGHT AGAINST THE STRONGHOLD OF WITCHCRAFT, IN THE NAME OF JESUS!

Contributed by Evangelist/Prophetess Artherrine Grimes Hoskins 11/2013

COMMAND THE MORNING
By Warrior Pastors Chris and Gina Inkum

Prayer 1

Every evil equation written in the cycle of the sun, moon and stars against me, my family and my loved ones, change in my favor in the name of Jesus.

Illustration - if someone sets a thermostat to 70 degrees, the unit will continue to work based on that programmed equation unless someone changes the setting to 75 degrees. 1+1=2 no matter where you go on this earth and regardless of the language. The only way the answer to any equation will change is if one of the variables in the equation changes. Unless you change a variable in the equation, your results will always be the same.

Prayer 2

Lord give me give me divine alertness to recognize divine opportunities in the mighty name of Jesus.

Explanation - Often times we are surrounded by a lot of opportunities we do not recognize. It is a tragedy to suffer hunger in the midst of plenty because of the inability to recognize opportunities. This prayer will open doors that are not visible to others and cause a divine breakthrough in your life.

Prayer 3
I take divine insurance and assurance against all forms of accidents and tragedy in the mighty name of Jesus. I decree and I declare that my loved ones and I will never ever become victims of circumstances and our steps are ordered of God.

Explanation - This prayer will cause you to be at the right place, at the right time, with the right people doing the right thing. The insurance policy of God is the only insurance policy without a deductible or limit.

THE BLOOD PRAYER
By The Global Prayer Network

Heavenly Father,

By the power and authority of Jesus Christ, I plead the blood of Jesus over my physical body, my soul and my spirit. I plead the Blood of Jesus over every demonic spirit that tries to oppress me and come against me. I plead the Blood of Jesus against every evil person who may try and attack me.

I plead the Blood of Jesus against any natural accident, almost accident and any catastrophes that may come against me or my family. I plead the blood of Jesus against any disease, viruses or illnesses that attempt to attack my body. In the name of Jesus, I will walk by faith according to 2nd Corinthians 5:7. I believe that the Blood of Jesus will protect me against all things that come my way.

Thank you, Lord! In the name of Jesus, I pray, AMEN!

WATCHMEN PRAYER
By Warrior Pastor Terrell Hunt

Father, I thank You for the divine assignment of a watchman and I receive and obey such a call with gratitude and humility. As a Watchman, I will cultivate my ability to hear the Holy Spirit and keep my heart pure so I can properly discern the areas You have assigned. Lord, I desire to pray Your purposes and protection over Your people, geographical area and/or nation.

I ask for dedication, focus, consistency, and perseverance as I discern and pray it into existence. I now ask You for insights and grace so I can pray effectively with a watchman's spirit. Father reveal the intimate needs of those for whom I should intercede. I will wait upon You, looking and listening to hear what You are saying. As a watchman on the wall I will always be on alert for any attempt of the enemy to attack or infiltrate my assigned area(s). I will not be unaware of the enemy's schemes to disrupt, destroy or divide.

Lord, I will stand, watch and station myself on the watchtower; and I will keep watch to see what You will say to me as I ask, Lord, what are You doing in my life, church, home, family, or city this day? Is there something Father You are calling Your people to do in cooperation with You? Father, whatever I do as a watchman no matter what it is, in word or deed, I will do everything in the name of the Lord Jesus and in dependence upon His love, power, and authority as I give worship and praise to Your name. Amen

WARFARE PRAYER POINTS FOR VICTORY
By Warrior Prophet Mark Korley

I call to resurrection every God given dream and vision in my life that the devil tried to kill.
I command every demonic womb to open up and release my blessings that it had swallowed up.

I command a release of my body, soul, and spirit from every satanic chain.
I undress myself of every satanic garment of poverty, defeat, reproach, and failure.
I put off every filthy rag from my life.
I unclothe myself of the spirit of heaviness.
I clothe myself with the garment of praise.
I clothe myself with God's robe of righteousness.

I am myself with God's armor of victory.
I invoke the supernatural, miracle working power of God.
I call into action God's right hand of righteousness to heal, deliver, and save my life and everything born out of my loins.
I activate God's warrior angels to fight on my behalf.

Oh Lord God of war, arise and let thine enemies be scattered.

Oh Commander of the Lord's army, arise in power and come to my rescue.
Let God's arrows of deliverance be released into my life and disperse all my enemies.
Let the fire of God descend down from heaven and consume every unclean spirit opposing my destiny.

PRAYER FOR FASTING
By Warrior Minister Crystal Bouldin
Matthew 6:16-18, Romans 12:1-2

Father in the name of Jesus, as according to Your Word, I declare a fast not obvious to men, but only to You. I seek Your face and revelation wisdom through Your supernatural power for my life, my family, my finances, my ministry, my business. I offer my body as a living sacrifice, holy and pleasing to You. Help me to grow to maturity, that my eyes will be enlightened to the hope of Your calling.

Reveal unto me Your purpose and plan for my life. I desire to experience a deeper more intimate relationship with you. To better focus in accomplishing and fulfilling Your perfect plan for my life. I pray as my body is cleansed by this fast, I am transformed by renewing of my mind that I may prove, what is that good, pleasing and perfect will of God. In Jesus' name. Amen.

PRAYER FOR HOPE
By Warrior Dr. Diana R. Williams

"For I know the plans I have for you," declares the LORD, "plans to prosper you and not to harm you, plans to give you hope and a future."

Jeremiah 29:11, NIV

Dear *ADONAI*, my Great LORD!

Thank *You ELOHIM*, the All-Powerful Creator for allowing each of us to come before You in prayer and praise! You are Good! You are Holy! You Are Faithful! We love You, Lord with all of our hearts, with all of our souls, with all of our minds, and with all of our strength. Thank You for loving us so completely and lavishly. Your love is extravagant and perfect towards us, so we celebrate You today! We thank You for this opportunity to come boldly to the Throne of Grace to utter this prayer of Hope.

We know that we must have hope if we want to live the blessed and abundant lives that You have planned for us. Your holy word urges all who put their hope in the Lord to be strong and courageous. According to Psalm 71:5, You are our hope, O Lord God! No matter what happens in our lives, we must remain full of hope as we recall that it is through

Your mercies that we are not consumed. Your compassions fail not. Great is Your faithfulness!

According to Romans 5:5, we also glory in tribulations, knowing that tribulation produces perseverance; and perseverance, character; and character, hope. Now hope does not disappoint, because the love of God has been poured out in our hearts by the Holy Spirit who was given to us. So we thank You Lord, for this hope. It is Audacious Hope, Earnest Hope, Faithful Hope, Glorious Hope, Patient Hope, Resolute Hope, Tenacious Hope, and Transformative Hope that anchors our soul. The Bible tells us in Romans 8: 24-25, NKJV, *"For we were saved in this hope, but hope that is seen is not hope; for why does one still hope for what he sees? But if we hope for what we do not see, we eagerly wait for it with perseverance."*

For those who have lost hope or have low hope, we ask that You restore their hope with renewed faith and confidence. Help them to remember that You delivered in the past, and made a way out of no way. You, Lord, turned what looked hopeless to something victorious so that we can look towards the future with hope. This hope is active and moves us forward even when we cannot see it. Therefore, please help us to hold fast to the confession of our hope without wavering.

Help us to remember that Your promises are sure! We declare, Dear Lord, that each plan that You have for us will manifest and we will thrive in triumph as hopeful people who have chosen to live victoriously. As we end this prayer, we thank You for the resurgence of hope, unrestrained joy, and the perfect peace that surrounds us at this very moment. It is in the mighty name of Jesus; we pray and declare it so! Amen.

"And, Now may the God of hope fill you with all joy and peace in believing, that you may abound in hope by the power of the Holy Spirit."
Romans 15:13, NKJV

PRAYER FOR HEALING
By Warrior Catherine Floyd

Jesus, You are the Word Who created earth, all creation therein, and all mankind. Thank You, Father for sending Your Word to heal us body soul and spirit. You are awesome in all Your ways. I bow down in Your presence. And I reach up and receive Your healing power.

We stand on Your Word. It will not return unto You empty. It will accomplish all that You want it to. It will succeed. It will prosper everywhere it is sent (Isaiah 55:11). Father, send Your Word and heal *(insert a name)* according to Your will, to Your great grace, and to Your mercy.

Almighty God, Lord, Savior and Healer, I praise You and bless You. Your grace and mercy You give daily (Psalm 103). Thank You for Your unfailing love and powerful miraculous acts (Psalms 107:19-21).

God exalted Jesus to the highest place and gave Him the name that is above every name, that at the name of Jesus every knee should bow, in heaven and on earth and under the earth (Philippians 2: 9-10). The name of Jesus is above the name of cancer, arthritis, diabetes, mental and emotional illnesses, and every other kind of illness, sickness, disease and pain. All must bow to the name of Jesus. You heal the brokenhearted (Psalms 147: 3). You heal all diseases (Psalm 103:2-4; Exodus 15:26; Isaiah 53:4-5). You hear and answer the cry of the righteous for healing (Psalm 34:17-22; Psalm 6: 2; Psalm 30: 2).

You protect and keep your righteous servant saints and restore them from illnesses (Psalms 41:2-3; Matthew 9:35). You shed Your Blood for healing all that concerns us body, soul, and spirit (Isaiah 53). Father God, because You sent Your Word and because of the shed blood of Jesus Christ, I ask You in the name of Jesus to heal *(insert a name)*. Let Your healing power flow through every internal organ, artery, vein, muscle, sinew, nerve, and bone from the top of the head to the soles of the feet. In the Name of Jesus, you are covered in His Blood, Amen.

PRAYER FOR HEALING FROM CANCER
By Warrior Gwelthalyn Huff

Heavenly Father, I believe I became a Cancer conqueror not because I went into remission but because I constantly renew myself and lifestyle. Your Word states in Matthew 15:13, "Every plant that my Heavenly Father has NOT planted will be pulled up by the roots." Cancer was not planted by God, death at the cross pulled sickness and disease up from the roots. I don't fail to remember cancer is a spiritual journey, making me aware, appreciative of everything, more grateful of every moment I have, more loving and kind, and dedicated to making this place better in Jesus name.

Thank you God, for healing me. It is in the mighty name of Jesus I pray, Amen.

DECREES FOR SUCCESS

The bible declares in Job 22:28, *"Thou shalt also decree a thing, and it shall be established unto thee; and the light shall shine upon thy ways."*

I declare that the peace of God will enter into my mind and destroy all confusion sent by the enemy according to Philippians 4:7.

I decree and declare that the joy of the Lord is my strength according to Nehemiah 8:10,
I declare that I will use wisdom when making decisions according to Proverbs 4:7.

I decree and declare that the plots of the enemy against me are canceled in the name of Jesus Christ according to John 10:10.

I decree that I am a blessing to the Nation(s) according to Malachi 3:12.

I decree and declare that my children are purpose-filled by the Lord according to Matthew 21:16.
I decree that no weapon formed against me will prosper according to Isaiah 54:17.

I decree that the healing hand of God will cancel every sickness or disease and replace it with wholeness according to Isaiah 53:5.

I decree and declare that I am no longer a victim but a victor in Jesus' name according to 1 John 4:4.

I decree that I can do all things through Christ which strengthens me according to Philippians 4:13.

I decree and declare that the generational curses in my life are broken from my life according to Matthew 11:29.

I decree and declare that I have the authority to bind every demon and ungodly spirit according to Matthew 16:19.

PRAYER FOR BUSINESS
Contributed by
Warrior Husband Harvey E. Hoskins, CPA

The Bible says you shall be the Head and not the tail, so say these prayers as you prepare to submit a Business Proposal to win profitable contracts. God will supply all of our needs. He promises to bless us and give us life more abundantly. When we understand God's mindset about riches, you will be amazed at the blessings that will overtake you.

- I claim the contract in the mighty name of Jesus Christ.
- Lord, hammer my matter into the mind of those who will assist me/us so that we do not suffer from demonic loss of memory.
- I paralyze the handiwork of household enemies and envious agents in this matter in the name of the Lord Jesus Christ.
- Let all my adversaries of my breakthrough be put to shame by fire in the name of Jesus Christ.
- I claim the power to overcome and excel amongst all competitors in the name of Jesus Christ.

- Let my/our decision by the panel be favored unto me/us in the name of the Lord Jesus Christ.

Read Joshua 1:9 before you attend interviews and submit contracts. Joshua 1:9, *"I have commanded you to be strong and brave. Don't ever be afraid or discouraged. I am the LORD your God and I will be there to help you wherever you go"* (CEV). Praise the Lord Jesus Christ for answered prayer(s). In the powerful name of Jesus I pray, Amen.

PRAYER FOR FAMILIES
By Warrior Pastor Deborah Holt-Foster

Our Lord, Our Mother, Our Father, Our Everything God,

Before You, Lord, we come heads bowed and some bodies bent with an expectation Lord, that You will hear our prayer. Lord, we are struggling in this season. Lord, we are confused in this season. Lord, we are hurting in this season. Lord, we are spiritually divided in this season. Lord, we have misplaced our love, our unity and our steadfastness in this season because many in our family don't have a relationship with You. When we don't have a relationship with You Lord, it's often difficult to have a relationship with one another.

Lord, as a family we pray for love, respect, acceptance, and unity. As a family, we plead the blood of Jesus over our family members who are scattered mentally, physically, emotionally, financially, and spiritually. We pray that in our mess, Lord that we will unite without hostility; that we will unite without selfishness; that we will unite despite our differences; that we will unite in love.

Lord, we pray that You will help us to forgive one another so that we may live healthy fulfilling lives because unforgiveness creates physical illness. Father, we pray that as we face each tomorrow that we would turn from our wicked ways and seek Your face. Lord, we pray that our family members who don't know You in the pardon of their sins will accept You into their hearts. Lord, we pray that each day continues to bring new mercies and new opportunities in You. Keep us grounded. Keep us steadfast, unmovable and always abounding in You. In Jesus' Name, Amen.

PEACE IN THE FAMILY

Contributed by Mother Artherrine Hoskins

Father, in the name of Jesus, I thank You that you have poured your Spirit upon our family from on high. Our wilderness has become a fruitful field, and we value our fruitful field as a forest. Justice dwells in our wilderness, and righteousness (religious and moral rectitude in every area and relation) abides in our fruitful field. The effect of righteousness is peace (internal and external), and the result of righteousness, quietness and confident trust forever.

Our family swells in a peaceable habitation, in safe dwellings and in quiet resting places. And there is stability in our times, abundance of salvation, wisdom and knowledge. There reverent fear and worship of the Lord is our treasure and Yours. O Lord be gracious to us; we have waited (expectantly)for You. Be the arm of Your servants our strength and defense every morning, our salvation in the time of trouble. Father, we thank You for our peace, our safety and our welfare this day. Hallelujah! Scripture References (AMP Isaiah 32:15-18 Isaiah 33:2,6

PSAM 91 *(Insert person's name you are praying for)*

_____ Lives in the shadow of the almighty, sheltered by the God who is above all gods. This _____ declares, that He alone is _____ refuge, _____ place of safety: He is _____ God, and _____ is trusting him. For He rescues _____ from every trap and protects _____ form the fatal plague. He will shield _____ with his wings. They will shelter _____. His faithful promises are _____ armor. Now _____ does not need to be afraid of the dark anymore, nor fear the dangers of the day; nor dread the plagues of darkness, nor disasters in the morning. Thought a thousand fall at _____. _____ will see how the wicked are punished but _____ will not share it. For Jehovah is _____ refuge! _____ chooses the God above all gods to shelter _____. How then can evil overtake _____ or any plague come near? For He orders his angels to protect _____ wherever _____ goes. They will steady _____ with their hands to keep _____ from stumbling against the rocks on the trail.

_____ can safely meet a lion or step on poisonous snakes, yes, even trample them beneath your feet! For the Lord say, "Because _____ loves me, I will rescue _____; I will make _____ great because _____ trust in my name. When _____ calls on me I will answer; I will be with _____ in trouble, and rescue _____ and honor _____. I will satisfy _____ with a full life and give _____ my salvation.
Contributed By Artherrine Hoskins

ENTERNAL LIFE
A breakthrough prayer for an individual who wants to know for certain they have eternal life

Key Scripture: "For God so loved the world, that He gave His only begotten Son, that whosoever believeth on him should not perish, but have everlasting life" (John 3:16)
Prayer: Dear God, thank you for sending Jesus to die for my sins. I believe in Him, and because I do, I accept your promise of eternal life. I am so grateful for your assurance that I will never perish. To me, Jesus truly is living water.
Father, I have sinned and fallen short of your glory, but you have commended your love toward me in that, even while I was a sinner, you gave me your

love through Jesus Christ. Thank you for your marvelous gift of eternal life.

I believe your Word, Father, and I receive the everlasting life you promise to me. I accept Jesus as being the living bread which came down from heaven, and as I partake of Him, I know I shall live forever. Thank you, Father.

My Savior, Jesus Christ, is the resurrection and the life. He is the way, the truth and the life for me. Because I live and believe Him, I know I shall never die. Thank you for forgiving all my sins. Jesus is the Lord, and I am a new creation. Old thinks have passed away. Now all things become new in Jesus' name. Amen.

Do you have the assurance that you will meet Jesus in peace?

PRAYER FOR MARRIAGES
By Warrior Antonia McLaurin

Dear Heavenly Father,

We come before You to thank You for all You have done and continue to do in our lives and marriage. We come before You today, God, asking for a stronger bond of unity and love in our marriage covenant. Father we ask that You give us the ability to love each other unconditionally while allowing nothing to come between us. Lord remind us daily of the love You showed us. You said in Your word "*But you commendeth your love toward us, in that, while we were yet sinners, you died for us,*" according to Romans 5:8.

Show us Your way of love daily. Help us, Father to recognize and work through anything that is not pleasing to You so we can constantly reach higher levels in our marriage – spiritually, mentally, and physically. Strengthen us so that we will resist the devil and draw closer to You and Your character. When we get upset with one another, remind us to look to You and Your peace and not to give the adversary any opportunities in our lives. As we work hard in our marriages, provide us with wisdom, discernment, knowledge and understanding that we make the best decisions as it relates to our marriage. Father, when we face difficulties in our marriage, let us know You are peacemaker. You are O Lord, a God of peace and not the author of confusion. Allow us to stand on the power of Your word that promises that You will keep us in perfect peace when our minds are stayed on You: because we trust You. We thank You, because You are trustworthy God.

We are thankful and excited to see the work of Your hand as we do our best to seek Your face daily. David stated in Psalm 27:3 that his heart said, *"Seek your face. your face, O LORD, I will seek."* Allow us to make every effort to keep ourselves united in the Spirit, binding ourselves together with peace. We love You, Lord and thank You for all these things. In Jesus' name we pray. Amen!

PRAYERS FOR FINDING A MATE

Father, I come before You in the name of Jesus, asking for Your will to be done in my life as I look to You for a marriage partner. I submit to the constant ministry of transformation by the Holy Spirit, making my petition known to You.
Prepare me for marriage by bringing everything to light that has been hidden — wounded emotions, walls of denial, emotional isolation, silence or excessive talking, anger, or rigidity **[name any wall that separates you from healthy relationships and God's love and grace].** The weapons of my warfare are not carnal, but mighty through You, Lord, to the pulling down of strongholds.
I know the One in Whom I have placed my confidence, and I am perfectly certain that the work, whether I remain unmarried or marry, is safe in Your hands until that day.
Because I love You, Lord, and because I am called according to Your plan, everything that happens to me fits into a pattern for good. In Your foreknowledge, You chose me to bear the family likeness of Your Son. You chose me long ago; when the time came You called me, You made me righteous in Your sight, and then You lifted me to the splendor of life as Your child.

I lay aside every weight, and the sins which so

easily ensnare me, and run with endurance the race that is set before me, looking unto Jesus, the Author and Finisher of my faith, Who for the joy that was set before Him endured the cross, despising the shame, and has sat down at the right hand of the throne of God. I consider Him Who endured such hostility from sinners against Himself, lest I become weary and discouraged in my soul. He makes intercession for me.

I turn my back on the turbulent desires of youth and give my positive attention to goodness, integrity, love, and peace in company with all those who approach You, Lord, in sincerity. I have nothing to do with silly and ill-informed controversies, which lead inevitably to strife. As Your servant, I am not a person of strife. I seek to be kind to all, ready and able to teach. I seek to be tolerant and have the ability to gently correct those who oppose Your message.

Father, I desire and earnestly seek (aim at and strive after) first of all Your Kingdom and Your righteousness (Your way of doing and being right), and then all these things taken together will be given me besides. So, I do not worry and will not be anxious about tomorrow.

I am persuaded that I can trust You because You

first loved me. You chose me in Christ before the foundation of the world. In Him the whole fullness of Deity (the Godhead) continues to dwell in bodily form **[giving complete expression of the divine nature]**; and I am in Him, made full and have come to the fullness of life **[in Christ].**

I am filled with the Godhead — Father, Son, and Holy Spirit — and I reach toward full spiritual stature. And He (Christ) is the Head of all rule and authority [of every angelic principality and power]. So, because of Jesus, I am complete; Jesus is my Lord. I come before You, Father, expressing my desire for a Christian mate. I petition that Your will be done in my life. Now I enter into that blessed rest by adhering to, trusting in, and relying on You. In Jesus' name, amen.

Prayers That Prevail Much Vol 1,2,3; Germaine Copeland, Tulsa, OK 1997

PRAYER FOR MOTHERS
By Warrior Mother Kathleen Talley

"Train up a child in the way he should go: and when he is old, he will not depart from it."
Proverbs 22:6, NKJV

Dear Heavenly Father,

We thank You for giving us the gift of our children. As mothers we also thank You for giving us the instructions in Your word on how to raise our children in the reverence and admonition of the Lord.

Lord, help us so we will be able to continue to raise our children according to Your commands in Your Holy Word. May it always be our first priority in our lives to live according to Your Son's, Jesus', example of obedience and honor to Your will as stated in Your word. In the Powerful Name of Jesus Christ our Lord and Savior, I pray. Amen.

PRAYER FOR MOTHERS
By Warrior Mother Gloria Wigfall

Dear Father,

I thank You for the opportunity You've given me, as well as all mothers, the gift of being moms. Dear Lord, as being mothers, help us from time to time to just stop and reflect on the many ways You've come through for us. The times when in our minds we felt so worn and torn to the point we just wanted to give up; knowing full well in our hearts that we would never ever give up on our children, as mothers willing and ready to go even beyond the last mile for them..

Father I thank You that You've given us wisdom to rest in You, as You replenished our souls. Strengthen us that we could continue on a little farther each day; until we witness our children grow into awesome young men and women, conditioned to go out and face the world. Father we understand even after they've reached adults, we're still moms, we're still thanking You, and will forever continue to praise You for covering them day by day with Your precious blood.

So Father. I thank You for the overflowing love, strength, and faith You've given us to face each day, and the courage to walk on, no matter what. Guide our thoughts that we continue to walk in peace, and gratitude of the honor of being mothers.

I pray, *"Above all else, guard your heart, for everything you do flows from it"*
Proverbs 4:23, NIV. In Jesus name, Amen.

PRAYER FOR CHILDREN AND YOUTH
By Warrior Pastor Chris Annan

Lord, we thank You for all the children and the young people who love You Lord and have accepted You as their Lord and Savior. We ask that You may continue to draw near to them as they have taken a leap of faith towards You, God. Father continues to guide their steps, as they walk through this world. Father never leave nor forsake them.

In their challenging times may they seek Your face God, and not try to rely on their own understanding. Lord, we also pray for the very lost souls of Your children. For those who are out there, contemplating their salvation, I pray for their peace, their comfort, and protection.

Father, wherever they maybe, as many as come forth, Father alter their life course, lead them to Your salvation. God, let them develop a spirit of humility God, so they may know that the fear of God is the beginning of their Wisdom.

Lord, I also ask that may You give Your children the strength and understanding to always fight the good fight, to always keep their faith, and to always finish everything they may start. Lastly God, I pray that may they always be at the right place at the right time, with the right people, doing the right things. In Jesus' mighty name we pray, Amen!

Prayer for Adult Children
By Mother Artherrine G. Hoskins

Father, in the name of Jesus, we bring our adult children before the Throne of Grace.
First of all, we ask You to forgive us for the times we have prayed for them with selfish motives and hindered Your answers to prayer. Forgive us for our self-righteousness attitude. Father help us stay mindful that it was not too long ago that we were bound in that old stagnant life of sin, but You embraced us with mercy, grace and love.

Thank You for the blessing of each child You have given us and for their unique purpose and destiny in life. We commit them to You and ask You to intervene in their lives at every opportunity today, revealing Your wonderful nature in new and fresh ways. Shine Your Heavenly light into areas of darkness and lead them on paths of righteousness and peace. We thank You for the infusion of the Holy Spirit in their lives through love, the fruit of the Spirit, for wisdom and revelation, and the Knowledge of You, Father God.

Create in our children pure hearts and renew a right spirit within them. Your Word in Nehemiah 4:14 states to fight for our children! Father, You are great and awesome and worthy to be praised. We fight for our sons, daughters, our spouses, and our houses in Jesus name. We thank You that Your promises are yes and amen and that You will contend with those who contend with us. And You will give safety to our children, save them and ease them day by day. You are Our LORD, Our Savior, Our Redeemer, and Our Rock!

Help our children in the selection of their friends. Please keep them from ungodly relationships. Give them keen discernment and may they hear Your voice and be quick to listen. May all our children repent and be baptized in the name of the Lord Jesus Christ for the remission of sins; and they will receive the gift of the Holy Spirit. Thank You for pouring out Your Holy Spirit upon our adult children now so that they can prophesy, so that our young men shall see visions. Father, create in them a love for Your WORD. Fill their lives with Your presence and guide their steps daily. Thank You, Dear Father, that our children are a chosen generation, a royal priesthood, and a holy Nation. Thank you Father for confirming Your WORD in them. We give You Glory, Honor and Praise. In Jesus name we pray. Amen.

Prayer for Un-Married
By Warrior Minister Desmarie Guyton

Lord, as I come to You, My Father who is in heaven, I humble myself at Your feet as Ruth did with Boaz asking and thanking You for covering me. I thank You, Lord, that all though I am not married in the natural, I am Your Bride in the spiritual who lacks nothing for You are my source that provides all of my needs. You are mine and I am Yours and Your love is the greatest love I have ever known. One that provides me comfort when I'm alone, yet I'm not lonely. Love that catches every tear when circumstances of this world have caused me to cry out to You. Love that has risked His life for me, died for me, and rose again for me that I may be set free and have a life with You, My Savior, as Your Bride.

I'm so grateful for Your love, and as I live in this world that is not my home. I ask You in the name of Jesus to keep me, Your Bride in the protection of You. Continue to lead me on Your path of righteousness so I'm not like silly women or men being led by fleshy desires or emotions which can bring me to the pitfalls of this world. But that I am constantly led by Your Holy Spirit, leading me beside Your still waters that bring restoration to my soul.

Let the refreshment of Your Holy Spirit continue to bring forth living water in my life as it pours out Your love for all to see. And let others stand in awe of Your beauty as I do, My Groom, My husband, My Lord and My Savior in which You have bestowed Your image upon me giving me Your name. Thank you, for Your love. Thank You for your wisdom. Thank You for all that You have given me, Your Bride. I will honor You and continue to give You all the glory now and forever. In the name of Jesus, Amen.

BEREAVEMENT PRAYER
By Dr. Peggy Enochs

(2 Corinthians 1:3-7)
To a most wise, loving, and caring Father, we honor you and bless your name. Thank you, Lord, that you are present with us today. Thank you that we can cast all our cares upon you. Thank you that you are touched by our infirmities. Thank you that you had a plan for our lives even before we were born. Thank you for the price you paid that we might have an abundant life. Thank you that you went to heaven to prepare a place for us. Christ in us, the hope of glory!

Today, dear Father we come to you on behalf of individuals, families, and friends who have lost loved ones through death. Maybe, it was a suddenly. Maybe, it was a natural death. Perhaps, there was a chronic or acute illness, or maybe, it was death by suicide. It could have been a stillbirth, an abortion, a miscarriage, a murder, or even the death of a pet. Maybe, some had to make a difficult medical decision for a loved one that ended in termination of life. Whatever the case, their heart is fractured; and, the grief is hard.

The pain is great, and at times, one feels an overwhelming tangled ball of emotions. Some are devastated and numb. Thank you, Lord, for the assurance that they are never alone in their state of sorrow, despair, grief, and all that it entails. Even in the Garden of Gethsemane, you felt overwhelming sadness and anguish praying, "My Father, if it is possible, let this cup pass me by." You even wept when Lazarus died. You know pain and sorrow. We thank you for the gift of being able to cry and release – to let go and to find comfort in a wise and all-knowing God. And, for those who have shattered beliefs about life, the world and even God, meet them at their point of need.

Thank you, Lord for the Holy Spirit, the great Comforter, and compassionate Helper and Companion, who will lead us through this healing journey as we call on Your great name.
Thank you, Lord, that weeping may endure for a night, but joy comes in the morning. Lord, send people across the paths of those grieving to bring divine comfort. May they choose God's Word and speak truth. May they know that it's okay to be silent.

Yes, their presence can mean so much more than many words. Send people given to acts of kindness, and people who will follow through for months after the initial loss. We thank you Lord for the heavy lifters who can assist one another with heart-heavy burdens of all kinds. We thank you Lord for the praying saints and for our great Intercessor making intercession on their behalf. For the bereaved, Lord, continue to surround them with your overwhelming love, strength, truth, rest, and peace that surpasses all understanding. Thank you, Lord, for new mercies every day. Thank you, Lord, that your compassion refreshes and refills every morning as you bring more mercy and grace into their life. You hear their cries, and you feel their pain. You can also see deep within their heart.

Have your way Lord! May they have a heart of gratitude even in their deepest sorrows. Cause them to think and ponder on the "good times" related to their loved one and to give thanks. May they be given a good dose of medicine – laughter - for it will bring healing for the spirit, soul, and body through the releasing of stress, improving their mood, boosting immunity, and relieving pain. And, Father, add a "now" word to encourage them to press their way through the maze of emotions in this journey toward divine freedom. Let them hear Your voice above the silence, the noise, and the pain.

Many things they may question, or they may not understand about the death of their loved one. May you rid them of the "woulda –coulda- shouldas" that could bring heartache and regrets. May they focus on Your character and who You are – the Great I Am. May they release their fractured hearts to You, a loving and faithful God. I pray, God, that they would not separate themselves from You, Father. Satan cannot steal their destiny. May their eyes be opened as they gaze upon you and their hearts fixed that they will walk this journey of healing out to Your glory.

Thank you, Lord, that there is no failure in You. Help them Lord to look past the pain and see Your glorious face clearly and unmistakably. May they be reminded that Your plans are good for them, not to harm them, but to give them a future and a hope. May they awaken in this hour for the provisions You have already made for their healing. I ask this prayer in Jesus' name. Amen.

PRAYER FOR WIDOWS
By Warrior Gloria Towner

A Widow's Journey

When you first start on this 'Journey of Widowhood', a life filled with unexpected changes and challenges, you are so stunned and numb, you really do not know what to do or expect. When you are a Christian, you believe and trust God. However, you must go through the 'Grief' Cycle Process. Part of that process is that you are 'angry'. Yes, even angry with God for taking your loved one but you do not stay there long. You will also 'rationalize' and 'bargain' with God before you actually 'recognize' God is LOVE and He loves YOU!

That God so loved the world that He gave His only Son to die for you (John 3:16). You then began to understand and accept and feel empowered to pray and to believe. God loved your loved one so much that your husband who also believed is not dead. He lives because of God's Son Jesus Christ. I

t is at this time that you will likely begin talking to God. Finding and reading words of encouragement opening up your bible and starting a journey of prayer, praise, and trusting God even writing a journal.

The Lord's Prayer and the 23rd Psalm usually becomes a familiar "point of reference" and brings great comfort. This begins for many as it did for me, a sustaining foundation in strengthening my personal relationship with God. The prayer I am submitting is one that encompasses these early days, months, and years of learning to pray. I would talk to God. Tell Him what was happening to me and seek His guidance.

I would thank Him and praise Him as I trusted Him to keep me and "bring me back to a life of living again!"

The PRAYER

Father God, in the name of Jesus, I come before You. First Lord, I want to thank You for getting me through another day. Thank You for the life my husband and I had together. Thank You for blessing and keeping us through the great times, good times, and the bad times. Thank You Lord for Your grace, goodness, and mercy.

Lord, I know Your word says that You will comfort those that mourn. That You are our Shepherd and we shall not want; that You sent Your word to heal the broken hearted and that You would never leave nor forsake us. That Your goodness and mercy will follow me all the days of my life. But Lord, right now, I feel so heavy and burdened down. My heart is broken like a part of it has been cut away and I am feeling so numb and alone. I have people around me. They are praying and trying to encourage me. I thank You for them.

But Lord this is _____(insert a name)____ talking to You, my Father. I am trying to speak and express some of these emotions. I know Your word says to cast all our cares on You for You care for us. I need to feel Your loving care, I need to feel Your presence Holy Spirit. I am feeling lost and alone without my husband (name). Lord I feel empty, devastated, and tired. I feel like my own life has come to a stop, a dry place, yet, I am crying wet tears one minute and trying to smile at the same time.

I am thankful for the people and my family who are trying to encourage me telling me everything is going to be alright. Lord, I know You are God and Lord over my life. You know what it is like to see someone You love die! After all, You gave Your only son, Jesus Christ to die for us. Lord I know because of Christ, death is not the end for those who believe. And I do believe You, God and trust You.

I believe in Jesus, who said to Mary and Martha, when their brother died, that He is the resurrection! Because of Christ, I can and will have the strength to endure and live an eternal life with You! Right now Lord, I need You to take my hand and uphold me with Your righteous right hand, pull me out of this valley and uphold me! Lift me up out of this miry clay, out of the valley of grief.

I believe Father, You will bring me out of this. You have done it for others and I know You are no respect of persons. I believe You are Jehovah Jireh my Provider, You can do anything but fail. I believe Your word that says:
- You will turn my mourning into dancing
- You will take off this heavy garment of grief and restore it with praise
- You will never leave me nor forsake me
- And you will give me joy for my sorrow

Holy Spirit, my Helper, help me make this exchange of restoration right now, in the name of Jesus! Lord Help me also to understand all the business, paperwork, insurance, the estate, and send honest and compassionate people who will also assist my family and me. Thank You God for meeting all our needs according to Your riches and glory through Christ Jesus.

Lord, as I am placing all these things in Your care, I am already feeling the presence of Your spirit and power. Thank You for being such a loving and attentive God. Thank You for Your peace and fresh anointing. To God be the Glory. I love You, Lord. I thank You. I praise You. Amen

WIDOWER'S PRAYER
By Warrior Rolene Love

Lord I thank you for your peace and comfort, for you know when we go through trials and struggles, and can barely see ahead of us, that you are already there with us.
You lift me up above my circumstances to a place of comfort and direction.
I Thank You Lord, that when I go through difficult times, that you will give me a greater sense of your comfort and in it I know that you are my refuge and strength.
Lord, you are the light of my life and a lamp upon my feet that can never be put out. No matter what I face in life the Holy Spirit is there to help me and direct my path.
Lord, I give you thanks in all things, knowing that you reign in the midst of it all, and that God shall supply all my needs according to his riches in Glory by Christ Jesus.
(Philippians 4:19).
In times of trials, Lord I pray for your added sense of presence. I will now rest in confidence knowing, leaning, and believing in you O'Lord.

In Jesus Name I pray, Amen.

Prayer for Female Clergy
By Warrior Pastor Pamela G. Kellar

Almighty Creator, thou who made heaven and earth. Thou who has brought us thus far on our way. Thou who has appointed us to serve Thee in a more excellent way. We praise and give thanks to You.

We thank You for strength and pray that You will grant us wisdom. We thank You O God for those You provided to us as mentors and friends. We thank You for our forerunners upon whose shoulders that we stand, who listened to Your call and turned a deaf ear to naysayers.

We pray for female clergy, women in ministry. Fortify us of God in Your grace, mercy and love. Teach us Your ways and lead us in a straight path. Teach us God to act justly, to love mercy and to walk humbly with You.

Expand our understanding of "worshipping You" so that our worship translates to service to mankind. Open our hearts to be doers of the Word by caring for those in need; by speaking for our brothers and sisters who are voiceless and to decree charity to the disenfranchised and marginalized.

Help us O God to not become oppressors to each other because of pettiness and jealousy but teach us to become a chain not easily broken. Let us become a chain linked in love, joy, peace, patience, kindness, goodness, faithfulness, gentleness, self-control and respect so that we can be a blessing to You and Your Kingdom. We present these petitions asking in the mighty and matchless name of Jesus. Amen and Ashay*.

***Ashay** is a word used in African American culture to mean "and so it is" or amen*

PRAYER FOR THE PRESIDENT
By Warrior Gloria Wise

Heavenly Father we pray respectfully for the President of our country, Donald J Trump and all those in authority throughout our land. I Peter 2:17 says, *"Show respect for all men [treat them honorably]. Love the brotherhood (the Christian fraternity of which Christ is the Head). Reverence God. Honor the emperor" (AMPC).* We pray with clear understanding that government authority is established by You, Father. *"Let everyone be subject to the governing authorities for there's no authority except that which God has established."* Romans 13:1a, NIV.

We also pray knowing God's Word says, *"the king's heart is like channels of water in the hand of the Lord, HE turns it wherever he wishes."* Proverbs 21:1, AMP. So we pray for him because Your Word says in I Timothy 2:1-3, "I urge, then, first of all, that petitions, prayers, and intercession and Thanksgiving be made for all people-for kings and all those in authority, that we may live in peaceful and quiet lives in all godliness" (AMP). This is good and pleases God our Savior. Help our President and all our leaders at all levels to accept wise counsel.

Teach our President to trust in You. Psalms 21:7 says, "*For the king trusts in the LORD; through the unfailing love of the Most High he will not be shaken" (NIV)*. .Protect him from the evil one. II Thessalonians 3:3 says, *"But the Lord is faithful and He will strengthen and protect you from the evil one."*(NIV). Give him direction, foresight, and understanding in making decisions. I Chronicle 22:12 says, "*May the Lord give you discretion and understanding when he puts you in command...so that you may keep the law of the Lord*" (NIV). Generously answer his prayer for wisdom. James 1:5 says, "*If any of you lacks wisdom he should ask of God who gives generously to all without finding fault and it will be given to him*" (NIV).

Pour out Your spirit on his leadership. Deliver him from opinions contrary to Your Word. Ps 119:105 says, "*Your Word is a lamp to my feet and a light for my path."* Protect him from harm and bless and protect his family. Psalms 21:11 says, though they plot evil against you and devise wicked schemes they cannot succeed. Ezekiel 6:10 also says, pray for the wellbeing of the king and his sons. Enable him to carry out his duties with humility towards you and towards others. I Peter 5:5b, NIV says, "*clothe yourselves with humility toward one another because God opposes the proud but gives grace to the humble.*" Bless him with strength, endurance, stamina. Isaiah 40:31 says, *"those who hope in the Lord will renew their strength, they will soar on wings like eagles, they will run and not be weary, they will walk and not be faint"* (NIV).

Equip him to act accordingly to Your will and to make choices pleasing to You. Give him courage to do the right thing even when urged to do the wrong thing. Proverbs 2:11-15, NIV says, *"Discretion will protect you and understanding will guard you- wisdom will save you from the ways of wicked men, from men whose words are perverse, who leave the straight paths to walk in dark ways, who delight in doing wrong and rejoice in the perverseness of evil, whose paths are crooked and who are devious in their ways."*

Give him a tender heart of compassion toward those he leads and serves. Colossians 3:12b, NIV says *"clothe yourselves with compassion, kindness, humility, gentleness and patience."* Let Your Holy Spirit draw him to Yourself Lord. May he surrender his life to You and become Your servant. May he lead Your people in the ways of Your Word. In the powerful name of Jesus, Amen

Prayer for the State
By Warrior Minister Crystal Bouldin
1Timothy 2:1-4, Matthew 16:19

I pray in the name of Jesus for every man, woman and child living in this State. From mountain top to valley low to every home, business, marketplace, church, mall, city hall, government and government agencies, parks and land in the state. We release the wisdom of God to fulfill Your plan in the earth and bless the people that we the body of Christ may live a quiet and peaceable life in all godliness and honesty. We lift up the State and our community unto You and declare the total and absolute victory over the works of darkness.

Satan, I bind you and command you to take your hands off this State and this community. Take your hands off the social, political and economic arenas. I set loose the power of God to accomplish the will of God in the land. Your kingdom come Your will be done in this State as it is in heaven. In the powerful name of Jesus, I pray, Amen.

PRAYER FOR THE NATION
By Warrior Minister Crystal Bouldin
2 Chronicals 7:14-15, Ephesians 3:20

In the name of Jesus, I lift up in prayer this great nation. This country was founded in the pursuit of freedom, liberty, justice and in God we trust. We, Your people come before You and humble ourselves, to pray and seek Your face. In agreement with Your word, we pray for this nation to turn from its wicked ways then You will hear from heaven, forgive their sin and heal this Nation.

You are our God, Almighty God, God of all the earth, Creator of Heaven and Earth, and able to do infinitely more than we ask or imagine. We stir up the power that worketh in us on the behalf of this nation for an awesome move of Your Spirit to disrupt, intervene, block and stop the enemy and his evil work in this nation. From sea to shiny sea. From north to south and east to west, we release Your glory, Your power, Your goodness and Your mercy. For thine is the kingdom and the power and the glory forever. In Jesus' name I pray, Amen.

PRAYER FOR THE NATIONS

Yolanda E. Shields
Minister, Author, Speaker and CEO

Heavenly Father we, pray, and intercede, with thanksgivings for all nations and people, including as well those that are in high positions of power in local and national government and other positions of authority.

Lord we pray that You would look down in grace and mercy on all nations. Guide them in Your grace that they may honor You in their nation, so that they may live a quiet, peaceful and godly life – that is honoring to You. Father we ask You to give wisdom to those who are responsible to make national decisions to establish national and local laws.

Lord we ask that You intervene in the decisions that are made in high places and especially pray that you would frustrate discussions and decisions that are made in secret places, which are outside of Your desires for all nations.

We disrupt the plans of men and women that wish evil and we pray that they turn them for Your greater good and for the benefit of those whom they serve.

Raise up a generation in all nations that will serve you. Lord give us an opportunity to serve nations because your word says in Psalms 2:8 "*Ask me to give you the nations and I will do it, and they shall become your legacy. Your domain will stretch to the ends of the earth*". We praise and thank You, in Jesus name I pray. AMEN

PRAYER FOR ISRAEL
By Warrior Sharon Mitchell

(Kindly note that devout Jews will not speak nor write the ineffable holy Name of God, but rather print it like this: "G-d". Therefore, out of reverence, I'll do the same in this prayer.)

1. Repentance and salvation for the Jewish people. We thank You, Abba (Father), for Abraham and his descendents, Your "Chosen People": *You chose Abraham* and his descendants, the Jewish people, because *Abraham chose You*! "He believed in Adonai (The Lord), and He credited it to him as righteousness"

(Gen. 15:6). May we Jews repent, forsake pride, and understand that it was only through Abraham's faithfulness and Your lovingkindness that we were "chosen". We thank You, Abba, that we were "chosen" for covenant with You, to be a light to the nations of the world (Deut. 14:2; Is. 42:6), and to have Messiah Yeshua (Jesus Christ), the true Light of the World (John 1:4, 9), come through our lineage for the salvation of all mankind. (Rom. 11:17; 1 Kings 2:45; Matt. 1:1-1; Rom. 10:9-11). What a privilege!

We repent for not having recognized, taken offense, rejected, and even disparaged our Messiah, who came to us first. (Rom. 1:16). As Yeshua said, "Father, forgive them; they don't understand what they are doing" (Luke 23:34).

We agree with Your plan, Abba, that "all Israel shall be saved". As the time of the "fullness of the gentiles" is unfolding (Rom. 11:25-27), we pray that scales are falling off our spiritual eyes, and You are touching our minds and hearts to know You and gain a clear understanding of Who our Messiah is: His purpose and true Identity in You. May we grow to recognize, honor, and love You, Yeshua (Jesus), "Arm of G-d" (Is. 52:10), Who became the "Lamb of G-d" and made propitiation for all of our sins. (John 1:29; Rev. 1:8; Is. 53). May we come to know the dual roles of our Messiah as both the "Suffering Servant" and the "Conquering King" (Is. 53; Rev. 19:11). "..the One who is, who was and who is coming" (Rev. 1:8).

2. The peace of Jerusalem and unity within her walls. "Pray for shalom (peace) in Yerushalayim (Jerusalem); may those who love you prosper" (Ps. 122:6). In the Name of Yeshua, Sar Shalom (Prince of Peace), we speak shalom to Israel's borders. We call forth shalom and godly unity within her borders, among her diverse citizenry:

Jews, Christians, Moslems, and all who reside there. (Ps. 147:14). May the Israeli governmental and political leaders find deeper understanding and new ways to work together for the good of the nation. May they fully understand that a house divided cannot stand. (Mark 3:25).

In the Name of Yeshua, we cut the lies of the enemy with the Sword of the Spirit and demolish all demonic strongholds of falsehood, witchcraft, offense, indoctrination, bigotry, anti-Semitism, hatred, murder, and all blood vendettas. (Eph. 6:12; Luke 10:19). We call forth reconciliation, through Your grace, of the Jewish people with all gentiles, Christians, Arabs, and Moslems. "When a man's ways please Adonai (Lord), he makes even the man's enemies be at peace with him" (Prov. 16:7). We call forth the revelation of the One True G-d, sincere repentance, heart changes, love, understanding, and unity among all people to bring forth an increased authentic, beautiful, multicultural Bride of Christ. Amen.

3. The Israeli Government, Military, and Society.
We thank You, Adonai, that godly "watchmen", Israeli citizens, the leadership, government, and military are vigilant and aware on every level, that we hear from Your Ruach HaKodesh (Holy Spirit or "Breath" of G-d"),and heed Your directives and

warnings. We thank You that "...the guardian of Isra'el never slumbers or sleeps." (Ps. 121:4), and we give thanks for the many miraculous military victories for us over the millennia! We pray for wisdom, discernment, and godly strategies for the government and military of Israel, including her Prime Minister (currently Benjamin Netanyahu), his cabinet, advisors, the Knesset (Congress), and all leaders in positions of power and influence in every area of Israeli society.

We thank You that Israel is a democratic republic (the only one in the Middle East at this time), and that she is a worldwide leader in medical breakthroughs, humanitarian advancements, and environmental and technological discoveries.

4. Reconciliation between Christians and Jews.
May my Jewish people come to understand that the atrocities committed against them over the millennia, under the banner of "Christianity", in the name of "Jesus", and by "Christian" nations, were not of You, Yeshua! May our misconceptions about true Christianity be cleared up. In March, 1998, Pope John Paul II apologized to the Jewish people for the passivity of the Vatican during the Holocaust. We pray for increased appropriate public repentance and sincere apologies for anti-Semitic attitudes and behaviors including

"replacement theology" (teaching that the Church has replaced Israel).

We especially repent for the lack of recognition and even outright opposition to Israel's Biblical and historical right to The Land, as ordained by You, Abba. (Gen. 15:18-21). May Your whole truth about the Middle East situation, in all its simplicity and complexity, come to light! May Christians and Jews alike have the conviction, courage, and wisdom, under Your direction and blessing, to staunchly and effectively stand for Israel when required.

May my Jewish people begin to see with new eyes and forgive. May legitimate, earned trust between the Jewish people and Christians be established. May we Jews ask for forgiveness for our resentments, fears, and distrust of gentiles. May we learn to fully trust only in You, Adonai, our Rock and our Redeemer. (Ps. 146:3-7).

5. Thanksgiving and sealing. We thank you, Adonai, for the privilege to partner with You as Your intercessors on behalf of the Nation of Israel. We know You hear and answer our worthy prayers. We give thanks and will continue to pray for Israel in accordance with Your will. We thank You for blessing those who bless Israel! (Gen.12:3). Amen.

BE BLESSED

Evangelist, Artherrine Grimes Hoskins

Now in closing, I just want you to know that I love each of you and there is nothing you can do about it because this love is being birthed from the third heaven, To my husband, children, spiritual children, grandchildren, spiritual grandchildren and children to come, nieces and nephews, sisters and brother, all the writers in this book and all my sisters and brothers all over the world, and to every reader of this book I love you, I bless you.

I pray for you and mention your name before the throne of grace every day. My most sincere prayer is that we all meet together with our Lord Jesus Christ. Stay close to Jesus and He will stay close to you. I pray for the bond of unity to be strong among us. I decree that any schisms and contentions among us will be broken quickly.

The LORD bless you and keep you; The LORD make His face shine upon you, And be gracious to you; The LORD lift up His countenance upon you, And give you peace. In the name of the Lord Jesus Christ. Numbers 6:24-26 Amen

ABOUT THE FOUNDER
The Power of Agreement Global Prayer Network

Evangelist Artherrine Grimes Hoskins is a Certified Spiritual Life Coach and recently (2019) completed the International Life Coaching Certification with special emphasis on mind, body, and spirit. Additionally, she is recognized as a Certified Holistic Life Coach (CHLC). She is a dynamic and motivating Inspirational Speaker, Trainer, Consultant, Workshop Leader, and Life-Changer, who has a desire to empower and coach women to different levels and dimensions of success and achievement in their spiritual, personal and professional lives. She is the Visionary Founder, and Overseer of the nonprofit organization Power of Agreement Global Prayer Network.

She and her husband are members of Bethel World Outreach Church. She has served as Prayer Team Leader for Power House Ministries. Evangelist Hoskins is a Spiritual Mother, Prophetic Intercessor, and Prayer Warrior. She is the National Prayer Coordinator for the National Consortium of Black Women in Ministry (NCBWIM). She received her Pastoral Psychotherapy and Chaplaincy Ministry

Instructions under the certification of Rev. Richard Reeves and Dr. Sandy Powell in 2010.

Evangelist Hoskins is a Board Member of the Interdenominational Services Organization of America, Inc. (ISOA) and a member of the Professional Woman Network (PWN), an international consulting organization dedicated to the empowerment of women and youth on a global basis. She is a Proverbs 31 woman, having been named one of the 100 outstanding women in Nashville, and recipient of the Patricia Harris Fellowship from Tennessee State University. She is a blessed mother of two, and a grandmother of six, and a devoted wife for over 43 years to Harvey Eugene Hoskins, CPA, and the reside in Nashville, TN.

Evangelist Mother Artherrine Grimes Hoskins

"When I received the Armor of God Prayer from the Power of Agreement Global Prayer Network, I felt both excited and challenged. It was another *"Test of Faith"* for me to follow the instructions about how to activate a new level of faith in my life by reciting the Armor of God prayer, commanding the day, and asking God to cover me in his precious blood daily."

**Dr. Jacqueline E. Davis
Princess Warrior- Northern Region July 2019**

Made in the USA
Monee, IL
28 March 2021